GREAT MOMENTS IN AMERICAN HISTORY

The Cost of Freedom

Crispus Attucks and the Boston Massacre

Joanne Mattern

rosen central
Primary Source™

The Rosen Publishing Group, Inc., New York

Published in 2004 by The Rosen Publishing Group, Inc.
29 East 21st Street, New York, NY 10010

Editor: Eric Fein
Book Design: Michael DeLisio
Photo Researcher: Rebecca Anguin-Cohen

Photo Credits: Cover (left), pp. 18, 22, 32 © Bettmann/Corbis; cover (right) illustration © Debra Wainwright/The Rosen Publishing Group; title page, p. 29 Library of Congress and Photographs Division; pp. 6, 30 © Hulton/Archive/Getty Images; p. 10 © Corbis; pp. 14, 31 © North Wind Picture Archives

First Edition

Library of Congress Cataloging-in-Publication Data

Mattern, Joanne, 1963-
    The cost of freedom : Crispus Attucks and the Boston Massacre / Joanne Mattern.— 1st ed.
    p. cm. — (Great moments in American history)
    Summary: Presents a version of the role Crispus Attucks played during the Boston Massacre and the Revolutionary War.
    ISBN 0-8239-4341-0 (lib. bin.)
    1. Attucks, Crispus, d. 1770—Juvenile literature. 2. African Americans--Biography—Juvenile literature. 3. Revolutionaries—Massachusetts—Boston—Biography—Juvenile literature. 4. Boston Massacre, 1770—Juvenile literature. [1. Attucks, Crispus, d. 1770. 2. African Americans—Biography. 3. Boston Massacre, 1770.] I. Title. II. Series.

E185.97.A86M38 2003
973.3'113'092—dc21
                                                                2003005204
Manufactured in the United States of America

CONTENTS

Though the American Revolutionary War began in 1775, the reasons for it went back many years. The English had placed high taxes on the people of its thirteen colonies in America. Many goods that the colonists needed in order to live became very expensive. The colonists asked England to stop taxing them but England refused. The colonists were unhappy. They wanted to be free of England's rules. The British government sent soldiers to the colonies to make the people obey laws.

In 1770, Boston was the largest city in the British colony of Massachusetts. There were many British soldiers in Boston. The people of Boston did not like having the soldiers in their town. This led to fighting between the colonists and the soldiers.

A man named Crispus Attucks was one of the people who were angry at the British. Attucks was been born a slave in 1723. His father was African. His mother was Native American. When he was twenty-seven years old, Attucks escaped from his master. He spent the next twenty years working as a sailor on different ships. In 1770, Attucks was in Boston after being out to sea where he had worked on a whaling ship. His arrival in Boston came as the tension between the British and the colonists was reaching its boiling point.

Attucks understood the colonists' desire to be free. As a former slave, he knew what it was like to be controlled by others. He joined the colonists in their struggle for freedom—and his actions made history. On a cold day in March 1770, Crispus Attucks became the first person to die in America's struggle for freedom.

Crispus Attucks was born and raised in Framingham, Massachusetts. He and his family were slaves. When he was twenty-seven years old, he ran away from his owner to start a new life.

Chapter One

TROUBLE IN BOSTON

On a warm night in Boston in September, 1769, Matthew Curry ate dinner in a tavern near the docks. The salty smell of the ocean came in through the open windows.

Suddenly, Curry heard a voice he knew. He looked up. A tall, strong man had come into the tavern. Curry waved. "Hello, Crispus!" he called.

Crispus Attucks smiled when he saw his friend. He came over to sit at Curry's table. "Hello, Matt. How are you?" he asked.

"I'm well. I haven't seen you in a long time," Curry answered.

"I was at sea," Attucks said. "We just arrived this morning. I will be in Boston for a while. I want to get a job here until my ship sails again."

"I've been working at a rope factory," Curry said. "I can get you a job. Many sailors work there when they aren't at sea."

Attucks smiled. "Thank you, Matt. So tell me, how are things in Boston?"

"Not very good." Curry said. "The British are worse than ever! Their taxes and laws are too much to bear."

"Are they still telling us we must pay taxes on sugar and tea?" Attucks asked.

"And other things—they even sent customs collectors to collect the taxes. The customs collectors make sure nothing comes in or goes out of the colonies illegally. They also make sure taxes are collected on all these goods."

"Why should we pay our money to the British?" Attucks said. "They are all the way across the ocean. We should keep our money here in America."

Curry laughed. "Many people feel the same way. A group called the Sons of Liberty is taking part in a boycott of British goods.

Even the ladies have stopped wearing British clothes. The British can't collect taxes if we don't buy their products!"

"Good idea," Attucks said. "I see a lot of British soldiers in town. Those red coats really make them easy to spot!"

"Some people call them 'lobsters.' The soldiers are here to protect the customs collectors and force us to obey British laws. There have been some fights between the British soldiers and the colonists."

Attucks's face grew angry. "I don't like it," he said. "I was a slave long ago, Matt. It is a bad life. Now it seems the colonists are slaves to the British. This can't go on. People need to be free. We must do something."

"Do you think people will fight a war for their freedom?" Curry asked.

"They will." Attucks's dark eyes narrowed. "And I will fight right along with them."

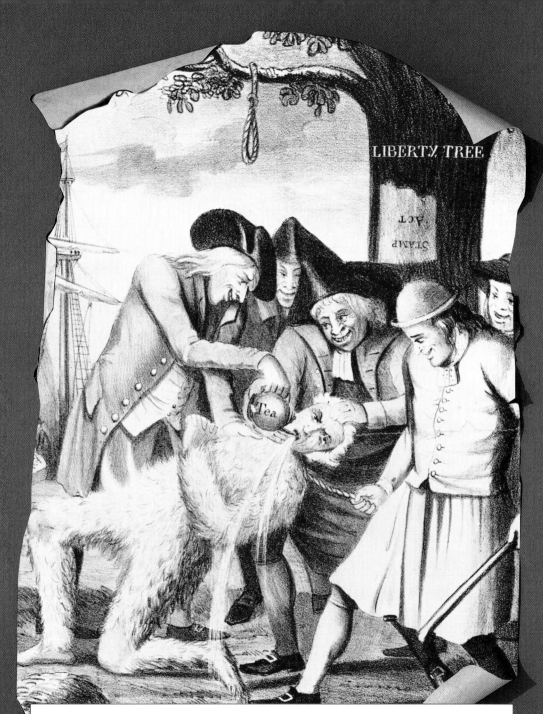

Boston colonists often fought with British tax collectors. This picture shows Boston colonists tarring and feathering a tax collector. When a person is tarred and feathered, they are first covered in sticky tar, then in feathers.

10

Chapter Two

DEATH IN THE STREETS

T he winter of 1769–70 was cold and snowy. For a part of this time, Attucks was at sea. When he came back to Boston, he and Curry worked at the rope factory.

The boycott of British goods continued. The Sons of Liberty painted signs on shop windows to tell people which stores were selling British goods. Sometimes groups of young colonists broke shop windows. This made the shopkeepers angry. They lost a lot of money because the people were not buying their British goods. Now their property was being damaged.

Attucks walked to work on the morning of February 22. Suddenly, he saw Matt Curry and their friend Sam Gray running toward him. "Did you hear what happened at Mr. Lillie's shop last night?" Curry asked.

"Some people put tar and feathers all over his windows," Gray explained. "Now a crowd is blocking the door."

Attucks and his friends rushed to Mr. Lillie's shop. They saw a large crowd outside. A man named Mr. Richardson came out of his shop next door. "Get away from our stores!" he yelled.

"Richardson won't take part in the boycott," Curry told Attucks. "He sides with the British."

People shouted at Richardson. The shopkeeper took a horse and wagon from someone in the crowd. He tried to drive it through the crowd. But the people would not let him. They threw rocks and sticks at Richardson.

Richardson ran inside his shop. Then he came back. He had a gun in his hand. He shot into the crowd. Two boys fell to the ground. Crispus could see that they were badly hurt.

"I know one of those boys," Curry said. "His name is Christopher Snider. He is only eleven years old."

The crowd rushed toward Richardson.

12

"Murderer!" they shouted. They took him to jail. Other people helped the two boys who had been shot.

Attucks and his friends returned to work. But they could not forget what they had seen that morning. While they were eating their lunch, a boy ran into the yard. "News! News!" he shouted. "Christopher Snider is dead!"

Attucks pushed his food away. "This has gone too far," he said. "Now, children are dying."

Attucks, Curry, and Gray went to Christopher's funeral. So did many other people in Boston. Four hundred boys led the march through the streets. Christopher's family walked behind them. More than two thousand people followed.

Attucks listened to the speeches at the funeral. One man said, "Christopher died for the cause of American freedom."

"And he probably won't be the only one to give his life for our just cause," Attucks whispered.

British soldiers were used to help collect taxes from the colonists in Boston. British soldiers were also located in the other American colonies, too.

Chapter Three

BELLS RING IN BOSTON

Attucks could not forget what had happened to Christopher Snider. His belief that the colonists should be free from the British grew stronger than ever. As the days passed, he spent most of his time talking to people in Boston. "It is time for the British to leave our colony," he said. Attucks was a smart man and a good speaker. His words excited the colonists. "We will not let the British make us slaves!"

Most people agreed with Attucks. They decided that the next time there was trouble, the church bells would ring. Church bells usually rang when there was a fire. Now they would ring to tell every-one in Boston that the time to fight had come.

On March 2, 1770, a British soldier came to the rope factory. Attucks heard him ask for work. "I'll give you a job," yelled one of the ropeworkers.

"You can clean my outhouse!" He was making fun of the soldier.

"Don't speak to me like that," the soldier said. He tried to hit the worker. A fight broke out but the workers chased the soldier away.

March 5 was a cold day. People gathered in the icy, snowy streets. They had a feeling something was going to happen between them and the British soldiers. For days, the people in Boston had been growing even more restless. The British soldiers were also becoming angry at the way the colonists were treating them.

That night, Attucks was eating dinner at a tavern near the Boston Customs House on King Street. Outside, a disagreement started between a soldier and colonists. Hugh White, another British soldier, stopped the fight and told the colonists to leave. But he was getting angry. One boy ran away with blood on his face. "The soldier hit me!" he screamed. "He tried to kill me!"

Attucks went outside to see what was going on. Just then, church bells began to ring all

over Boston. Crispus felt his heart thumping. The time to fight for freedom was now.

Attucks watched people gather in front of the customs house. A few boys threw snowballs at Hugh White. "Lobster!" they shouted at him. "Get out of Boston!"

White held up his gun. "Go back to your homes!" he shouted.

"The British are the ones causing trouble!" Attucks shouted back. "Go back to England and let America be free!"

From down the street, some British soldiers heard the shouting. Their leader, Captain Preston, and eight soldiers rushed to help White. The soldiers pushed through the crowd with their sharp bayonets. They used these blades to push through the crowd. The crowd threw snowballs and pieces of ice at them.

"I'm going to get my friends," Attucks yelled as he ran to the docks. "We all must fight for freedom!"

This painting of the Boston Massacre was made by Henry Pelham, only two weeks after the event. Attucks (center) is shown being shot by a British soldier.

Chapter Four

MASSACRE!

When Attucks reached the docks, he called to his friends. "Matt! Sam! Come with me to King Street! The British are attacking!" He grabbed a stick to use as a weapon.

"What's going on?" Curry asked.

"There's a crowd at the customs house," Attucks explained. "The British soldiers are there with guns and bayonets." The men dropped their work and joined him. Attucks ran back to King Street. Behind him was a crowd of about fifty men. Curry and Gray had to run fast to keep up with Attucks.

When the group reached King Street, there was already a large crowd. Many of the colonists carried sticks and clubs. Captain Preston stood in front of the British soldiers. "Do not fire!" he ordered.

Attucks, Curry, and Gray pushed their way to the front of the crowd. "Are you afraid to fight?" Attucks yelled at the soldiers. "We are not afraid! We will fight for our freedom!"

Suddenly, someone in the crowd threw a wooden club at the soldiers. The club hit a soldier in the face. He fell to the icy ground. Then he jumped to his feet, raised his gun, and fired into the crowd.

The colonists rushed forward, attacking the soldiers. The colonists used snowballs, ice, rocks, sticks, and clubs as weapons. Shots rang out as several soldiers fired their guns into the crowd.

One shot hit Attucks in the chest. He screamed and leaned on his stick to stay on his feet. Curry rushed to his side. Before he could help his friend, another shot rang out. It also struck Attucks in the chest. He fell to the ground.

Curry lay down beside his friend. "Crispus!" he screamed. "He's dead!" Curry heard another shot. Sam Gray was shot dead.

"Stop firing!" yelled Captain Preston. Suddenly, everything was quiet. The fight was over. Eleven colonists had been shot. Four, including Crispus Attucks and Sam Gray, were dead. A fifth would die later.

A man named Benjamin Burdick helped Curry to his feet. Burdick looked at Attucks. "I'm sorry about your friend," he said to Curry.

Then he walked up to Captain Preston. "I want to see your face," Burdick said. "I hope the next time I see you is in a court of law. This night will not be forgotten."

Captain Preston marched his men out of the square. The colonists took care of the dead and injured. Curry guessed there were at least one thousand people in the crowd. Many were shocked by what had happened. They knew today's fight was done, but that their fight for freedom had just begun.

John Adams defended Captain Preston for the murder of Attucks. Adams also played an important part in the colonies' fight for freedom. After the war, he became the second president of the United States (1797-1801).

Chapter Five

TRIALS AND HONORS

C rispus had no family in Boston. Matt Curry helped bring his body to Faneuil Hall. Over the next three days, thousands of people came to Faneuil Hall to honor Attucks with speeches. They called him a hero.

On March 8, there was a funeral for Attucks, Sam Gray, and the other men who had died. People started calling the night of March 5 the Boston Massacre. Curry joined twelve thousand people as they walked up King Street. Some of the people were men who had worked with Attucks and the others.

Everyone marched to the cemetery. All the victims were buried in one grave. Curry was surprised to see Attucks buried with the others. "I thought only white people are buried here," he whispered to the man standing next to him.

"That's true. But Crispus is a hero. All heroes should be buried together."

After the funeral, Curry went to a tavern with some friends. The tavern owner had news. "Captain Preston and his men have been arrested for murder. John Adams has agreed to defend them in court."

"John Adams!" Curry exclaimed. "But he is a patriot, like us."

The owner shrugged. "Adams says everyone should have a fair trial."

The trial of Captain Preston did not begin until October 24, 1770. Curry went to court every day. He heard many people talk about Attucks. Some said he was a hero. Other people who sided with the British soldiers said he had started the fight.

A slave named Andrew described what he had seen. Andrew had been in the crowd on King Street on March 5. "I threw some ice at the soldiers," he said. "Then Crispus Attucks arrived. There were a lot of men with him. They had sticks and clubs. I saw Attucks try to

hit Captain Preston with his stick. Then he hit another soldier."

When it was his turn to speak, Curry said that Andrew's story was not true. "Crispus Attucks did not hit any soldiers. He was arguing with them. Then they shot him twice in the chest."

John Adams talked about Crispus Attucks. Matt could not believe Adams's words. "Attucks was a big man. He was a rough man," Adams said. "He knew how to fight. The soldiers thought Attucks wanted to hurt them. That is why they fired their guns. They were trying to save their lives."

Captain Preston spoke too. He said that the colonists had threatened to kill Hugh White. "The soldiers had to fire at the crowd to protect themselves."

The trial ended on October 30. It was decided that Captain Preston shouldn't be blamed for what had happened. The court decided that he had been protecting himself from the crowd. At the end of November, the eight British soldiers had their trial. Once

again, John Adams said the soldiers were protecting themselves. At the end of the trial, six of the soldiers were found innocent. Two others were found guilty of manslaughter.

After the trial, Matt Curry went up to John Adams. "I respect you as a patriot, Mr. Adams," he said. "But I cannot believe your words against Crispus Attucks."

Adams nodded. "I agree that Attucks meant well. But violence does not solve problems. It only leads to more violence."

"There will be more violence because of the Boston Massacre," Curry said. "I believe there will be a war."

"I believe so too," Adams said. "I can only hope that something good will come out of it."

Curry walked out into the cold, fall afternoon. *Crispus Attucks is a hero,* he thought. *The cost of freedom is high and he paid the price for it with his life. I know people will remember him and his deeds for many years to come.*

GLOSSARY

bayonets (BAY-uh-net) long knives that can be fastened to the end of rifles

boycott (BOI-kot) to refuse to buy something or to take part in something as a way of making a protest

colonies (KOL-uh-neez) territories that have been settled by people from another country and are controlled by that country

independent (in-di-PEN-duhnt) free from the control of other people or things

manslaughter (MAN-slaw-tur) the crime of killing someone without intending to do so

massacre (MASS-uh-kur) the brutal killing of a very large number of people, often in battle

outhouse (OUT-houss) an outdoor bathroom

patriot (PAY-tree-uht) someone who loves his or her country and is prepared to fight for it

slave (SLAYV) someone who is owned by another person and thought of as property

weapon (WEP-uhn) something that can be used in a fight to attack or defend, such as a sword, gun, knife, or bomb

Primary Sources

To learn about the past, we can study many different sources. Old letters, diaries, maps, and paintings are some of the sources that tell us about the people and events of long ago. The picture on page 29 was done by the famous American patriot Paul Revere. It shows the British troops firing on the American colonists during the Boston Massacre. Just as the witnesses at the trial of the British soldiers gave their different views of what happened, this picture shows the event from the artist's point of view.

The handbill on page 32 was written shortly after the Massacre. It tells us how angry the colonists were about the event. By reading the handbill, we can evaluate the mood of the colonists during this time. The handbill also shows us how information and opinions were spread during colonial times.

This picture of the Boston Massacre was done by Paul Revere. Revere was an important Boston patriot. This picture was printed in the March 12, 1770, issue of the *Boston Gazette* newspaper.

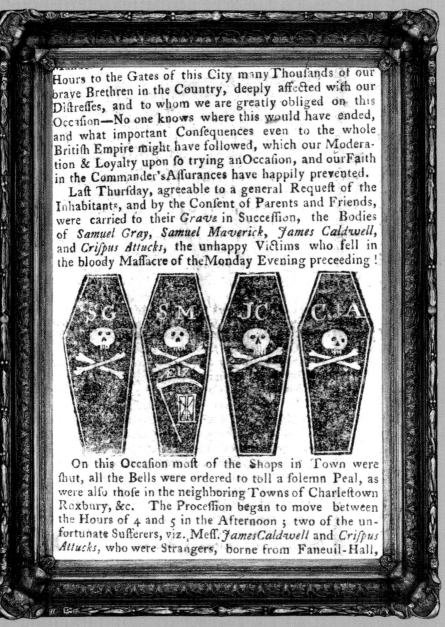

Hours to the Gates of this City many Thousands of our brave Brethren in the Country, deeply affected with our Distresses, and to whom we are greatly obliged on this Occasion—No one knows where this would have ended, and what important Consequences even to the whole British Empire might have followed, which our Moderation & Loyalty upon so trying an Occasion, and our Faith in the Commander's Assurances have happily prevented.

Last Thursday, agreeable to a general Request of the Inhabitants, and by the Consent of Parents and Friends, were carried to their Grave in Succession, the Bodies of *Samuel Gray, Samuel Maverick, James Caldwell,* and *Crispus Attucks,* the unhappy Victims who fell in the bloody Massacre of the Monday Evening preceeding !

On this Occasion most of the Shops in Town were shut, all the Bells were ordered to toll a solemn Peal, as were also those in the neighboring Towns of Charlestown Roxbury, &c. The Procession began to move between the Hours of 4 and 5 in the Afternoon ; two of the unfortunate Sufferers, viz. Mess. *James Caldwell* and *Crispus Attucks,* who were Strangers, borne from Faneuil-Hall,

Many Boston newspapers printed angry stories about the Boston Massacre. This article uses drawings of coffins to show four of the five people who died at the massacre. The "C. A." on the coffin on the right stands for Crispus Attucks.

After the Boston Massacre, the patriot Samuel Adams (pointing) demanded that Massachusetts governor Thomas Hutchinson remove the British soldiers from Boston. A cousin of John Adams, Samuel Adams became the governor of Massachusetts from 1794 to 1797.

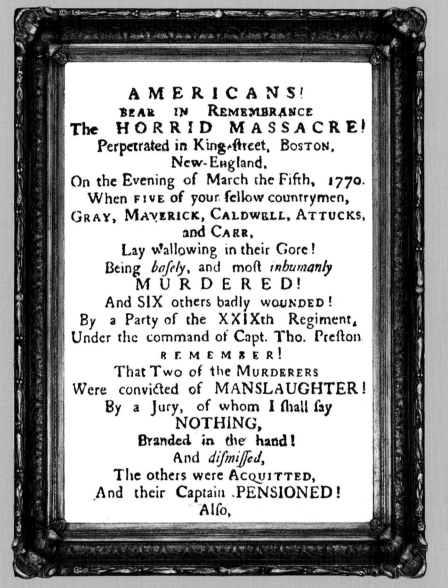

AMERICANS!
BEAR IN REMEMBRANCE
The **HORRID MASSACRE!**
Perpetrated in King-ſtreet, BOSTON,
New-England,
On the Evening of March the Fifth, 1770.
When FIVE of your fellow countrymen,
GRAY, MAVERICK, CALDWELL, ATTUCKS,
and CARR,
Lay wallowing in their Gore!
Being *baſely*, and moſt *inhumanly*
M U R D E R E D !
And SIX others badly WOUNDED!
By a Party of the XXIXth Regiment,
Under the command of Capt. Tho. Preſton.
REMEMBER!
That Two of the MURDERERS
Were convicted of MANSLAUGHTER!
By a Jury, of whom I ſhall ſay
NOTHING,
Branded in the hand!
And *diſmiſſed*,
The others were ACQUITTED,
And their Captain .PENSIONED!
Alſo,

Many handbills, or flyers, telling about the Boston Massacre were
printed and read by people in the colonies. These handbills were used
to remind the colonists about the horrible events that happened on
March 5, 1770.